MW01332426

Heyyy Family, Let's Write Your Future, Set Goals, Plan and Let's Refresh and be Trauma Free. Write your Dreams, See God's Success Manifest in Your Life, Career, and Business.

We love to collaborate. Share pictures of you using your journal/workbook and success stories about your life.

About The Author

LaKeisha Pope is passionate about mental health, advocating, coaching, and empowering people, to discover their inner selves through personal and professional growth. As The Founder of Royalty Counseling LLC, a multidimensional private practice and mental health coach. It's my goal to direct clients to embrace what God says about your mental health. Lakeisha is an active member of the Florida Mental Health Counselor Association, National Alliance on Mental Illness, an active Herbassador of the HERpernuer Network. LaKeisha Pope is a dedicated advocate, and compassionate person.

✉ Keisha@royaltycounselingllc.com
🌐 www.royaltycounselingllc.com
📷 rcounselingllc
🅕 LaKeisha Pope-Royalty Counseling

Refreshed & Trauma
FREE

THIS WORKBOOK/JOURNAL BELONGS TO:

_____

> WRITE AN AFFIRMATION, SCRIPTURE, OR QUOTE THAT ENCOURAGES YOU TO FINISH YOUR GOALS AND SEE YOUR VISION THROUGH UNTIL THE END.

Adverse childhood experiences, also knowns as ACEs, are adverse (negative and impactful) experiences that occur during formative childhood years. These include abuse, neglect and household dysfunction.

ACEs Assessment

Answer the following question **YES** or **NO** at any point while growing up during the first 18 years of life:

1. Did a parent or other adult in the household often: Swear at you, insult you, put you down, or humiliate you? Or act in a way that made you afraid that you might be physically hurt? **YES or NO**

2. Did a parent or other adult in the household often: Push, grab, slap, or throw something at you? Did a parent or other adult hit you so hard that you had a mark or were injured? **YES or NO**

3. Did an adult or person at least five(5) years older than you ever: Touch or fondle you or have you touch their body in a sexual way? Or Tired to or actually have oral, anal or vaginal sex with you? **YES or NO**

4. Did you often feel that: You didn't have enough to eat, had to wear dirty clothes, and had no one to protect you? Were your parents were too drunk or high to take care of you or take you to the doctor if needed or to school daily? **YES or NO**

5. Did you often feel that: No one in your family loved you or thought you were important or special? Or your family didn't look out for each other, feel close to each other, or support each other? **YES or NO**

6. Were your parents ever separated or divorced? **YES or NO**

7. Was your parental figure: Often pushed, grabbed, slapped, or had something thrown at them or sometimes either often kicked, bitten, hit with a fist or hit with something hard? Was your parental figure repeatedly physically harmed or threatened with a gun or knife? **YES or NO**

8. Did you live with anyone who was either a problem drinker or alcoholic or who used street drugs? **YES or NO**

9. Was a household member depressed or mentally ill or did a household member attempt suicide? **YES or NO**

10. Did a household member go to jail or prison? **YES or NO**

Add up the YES Score=

PRAYER CHANGES YOUR MINDSET

Write Your Own Prayer Request Below

Your Name: _____

For we walk by faith, not by sight (KJV)

~ 2 Corinthians 5:7

Dear Old Me

Write A Letter To Your Younger Self

_____
_____
_____
_____
_____
_____
_____
_____
_____
_____
_____
_____
_____
_____
_____
_____
_____
_____
_____
_____
_____
_____
_____
_____
_____
_____
_____
_____
_____
_____
_____
_____
_____
_____
_____

Therefore, if anyone is in Christ, he is a new creation; the old has gone, the new is here!

~ 2 Corinthians 5:17 (NIV)

I am resilient and capable of

HEALING

from my childhood trauma.

I deserve

LOVE,

understanding, and compassion.

How has your trauma shaped your beliefs about yourself?

_____

_____

_____

_____

_____

_____

_____

_____

_____

_____

_____

_____

_____

_____

_____

_____

_____

_____

_____

_____

_____

Strategies and Self-Care Practices

James 4:3

Describe a specific event from your childhood that still affects you today.

Strategies and Self-Care Practices

Mark 9:17-24

I am
WORTHY
of a happy and fulfilling life.

I am not defined by my past; I am
CREATING
a brighter future.

Be Gone... Anxiety

Dear Heavenly Father,

Thank You for being an overcoming God! I know I can take heart because you have overcome the world. Empower me to rise above my circumstance. Help me cast my anxiety on YOU because YOU care for me. Give me your power to overcome. Thank you for giving me the VICTORY! In Jesus' Name, Amen.

Philippians 4:4-7 and Isaiah 41:10

ESCAPING THE *Cycle of Anxiety*

You can reverse the vicious cycle of anxiety and create a positive cycle for yourself. One important step in this cycle is gradually confronting feared situations. This will lead to an improved sense of confidence, which will help reduce your anxiety and allow you to go into situations that are important to you.

CONFRONT — *feared situations without aid of safety behaviors*

INCREASE — *in anxiety for the short term but increase in awareness of physical sensation, thoughts and desired outcome*

COPING — *skills reduce anxiety to a level that is more manageable*

BELIEF — *in understanding how you can respond and cope with anxiety*

Anxiety & Stress

Experiencing an overwhelming emotion that is characterized by feelings of tension, worried thoughts, and physical changes will keep you on edge, fatigued, which makes it difficult to concentrate or even disturb your sleep. You may be experiencing anxiety which can range from mild to severe. Anxiety can be a reported problem if you recognize that you have been worrying a lot about insignificant situations or relatively harmless situations. Anxiety can become intense or overwhelming once it affects your relational, occupational, social, or educational/work functioning.

Stress can be defined as any changes that cause physical, emotional, or psychological strain. Stress is your body's response to anything that requires attention or actions. To some degree, we all experience stress. Your overall well-being to the response of stress makes a big difference.

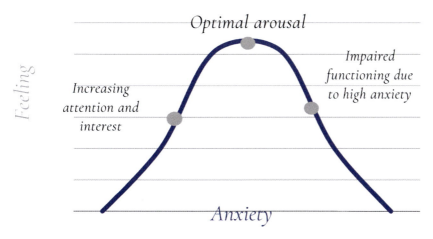

Do not be anxious about anything, but in every situation by prayer and petition, with thanksgiving present your requests to God.
~Philippians 4:6-7 (NIV)

JOURNAL *Anxiety & Stress*

For God did not give us a spirit of timidity but a spirit of power, love and self-discipline.

~2 Timothy 1:7 (NIV)

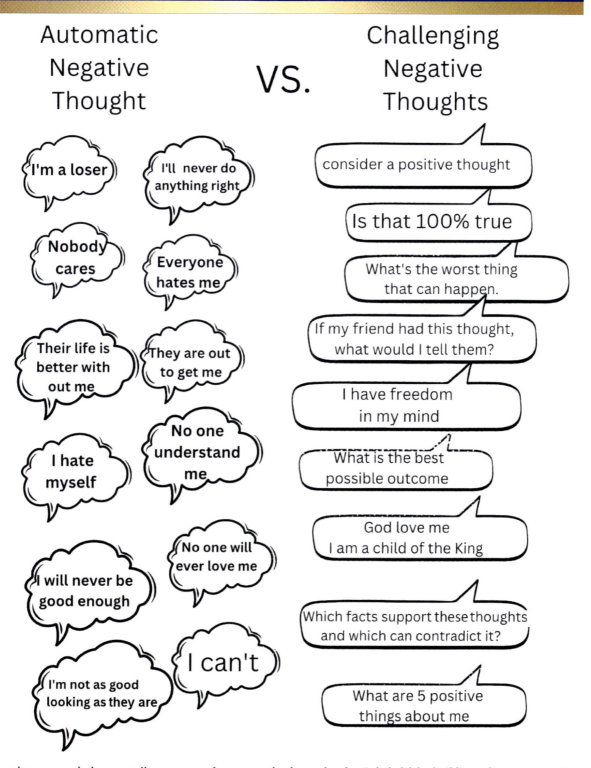

Do not let any unwholesome talk come out of your mouths, but only what is helpful for building others up according to their needs, that it may benefit those who listen.

~ Ephesians 4:29 (NIV)

Break Negative Thinking

Depression, anxiety and poor self-esteem are often the results of negative and irrational thoughts. Challenging irrational thoughts and bringing awareness of our thinking can really help us grow in every area of life!

1 *Is there substantial evidence for my thought?*

2 *Is there evidence contrary to my thought?*

3 *Am I interpreting without evidence?*

4 *What would a friend think about this situation?*

5 *If I view the situation positively, how is it different?*

6 *Will this matter after five years?*

OVERCOMING
Negative Thinking

Select a negative thought:

What triggered the negative thoughts?

How did the negative thought make you feel?

How distressing is this through?
- ☐ Mild
- ☐ Moderate
- ☐ High
- ☐ Other

_____
_____
_____
_____

Pick a negative thought:

Pick a negative thought.

What would you say to a friend in the same position?

Re-write this negative thought kindly.

How does this new thought make you feel?

RECOGNIZING Stress

1 List the ways you experience stress physically, emotionally and behaviorally.

Physically   Emotionally   Behaviorally

2 Circle the way stress affects you that are most troubling.

3 Lists things you can do to reduce the symptoms of stress. If you need ideas, think of activities where these symptoms are naturally lower (e.g. hobbies).

Too Blessed to be Stressed
How to manage your Stress

Stress is a part of our daily lives; however, it's important to control it in a healthy way to avoid negative effects on your physical, emotional or mental health.
It's important to control it in a healthy way.
Here are some suggestions for managing stress.

1. Identify the source of your stress.
Ask yourself Who, What, When Why questions

Talk About It…

2. Adjust and maintain a healthy lifestyle
Reduce or stop smoking and drinking. Get your body moving. Identify something new to read.

Talk About It…

3. Make time for fun and relaxation! Watch a movie!

Talk About It…

STRESS
Management

What is stress management?

Stress management is defined as the tools, strategies, or techniques that can reduce stress and reduce the negative impact stress has on your emotional, mental or physical well-being. When stress management is used regularly and in response to stressful life events, we can optimize our well-being

What are your five stress buttons (triggers)?

Stress happens when you have:
- A lot of things happening all at once
- An important decision to make
- A major event or life adjustment
- Something really dangerous happened to you or others

Where do you feel stress in your body?

Mark the areas with a black pen.

What helps?

Understand your stress buttons. Take, breaks and pause sometime. Listen to music. Keep a stress journal. Watch a movie!

GRATITUDE *Tracker*

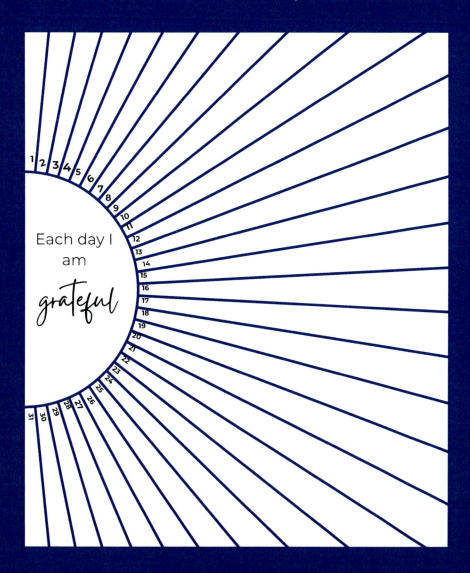

Give thanks in all circumstances, for this is God's will for you in Christ Jesus.

~ 1 Thessalonians 5:18 (NIV)

Values & Vision

MY VISION FOR THE NEW ME

Physical:

Spiritual:

Mental:

Relational:

Professional:

Financial:

Recreational:

And the Lord answered me, and said, write the vision and make it plain upon tables, that he may run that read it.

Habakkuk 2:2 (KJV)

Dear Future Me
Write a Letter To Your Future Self

Where there is no vision, the people perish: but he that keepeth the law, happy is he.
~ Proverbs 29:18 (KJV)

I have the
strength
to overcome any challenges that come my way.

I am
worthy
of healthy and supportive relationships.

BIBLE EMOTIONS WHEEL

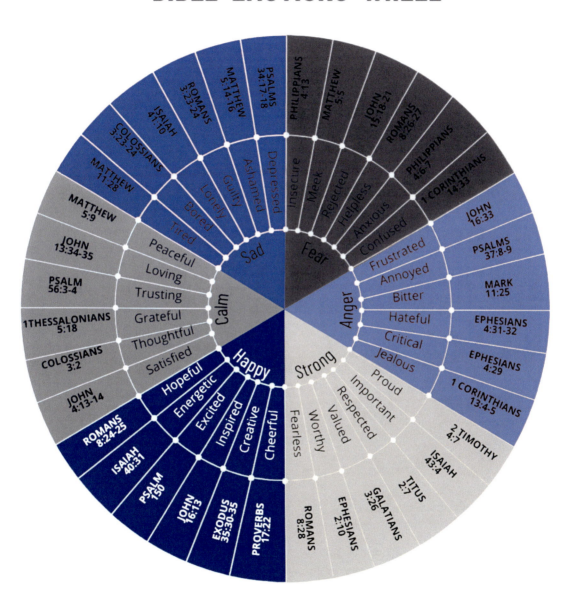

Trackers & Worksheets

COGNITIVE *Distortion*

Cognitive distortions are internal mental filters or biases that increase our misery, fuel our anxiety, and make us feel bad about ourselves. Our brains are continually processing lots of information. To deal with this, our brains seek shortcuts to cut down our mental burden.

Over Generalization
Drawing conclusions based on very few data points

Polarized Thinking
When you think that something can only be right or wrong

Mental Filtering
Turning your positive thoughts into negative ones

Minimizing and Maximizing
Exaggerate certain aspects of themselves or others while downplaying others

Blaming
Blaming others for everything and feeling like a victim

Personalization
Thinking all actions are directed towards you. Taking everything personally

Labelling
Judging yourself or someone else based on one event

Emotional Reasoning
Basing judgments on your emotions. Anything that feels right must be true

Should Statements
Should and should not statements are used to create pressure

For as he thinks within himself, so he is.
~Proverbs 23:7 (NIV)

DAILY
Self-care check in

A self-care plan is an intentionally constructed guide to promote individual health and wellbeing. This plan uses the notion that humans are life-long learners; and assists the user to build the required knowledge, skills, and attitudes to support their wellbeing.

Morning Check-in
Start your day with your morning routine. Build a routine that you enjoy doing and start your day doing things that will energize you.

Morning Time With God (Prayer)

Post-Work Wellness

- Assess your daily physical wellness
- Think about your daily intellectual wellness
- Consider your vocational wellness
- Consider your social wellness
- Look after your emotional wellness
- Assess your daily spiritual wellness
- Look after your financial wellness

Evening
- Follow an evening routine that grounds and relaxes you
- Think of wellness practices you will follow tomorrow

Habit Tracker

	🙏	💊	🍬	✗	🏃	🥤	$	🕐	👨‍👩‍👧	zᶻᶻ

HABIT Tracker

MONTH OF:

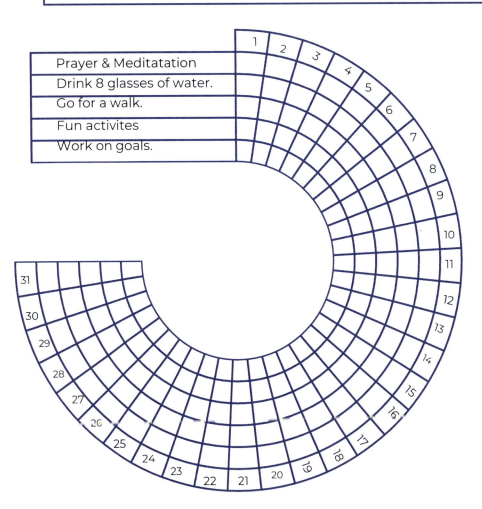

- Prayer & Meditatation
- Drink 8 glasses of water.
- Go for a walk.
- Fun activites
- Work on goals.

The secret to your success is found in your daily routine.

SELF-CARE
Daily Check-In

Self-care means really listening to your body, taking moments to check in, intentionally tuning into the thoughts going on in your mind. Challenging your behaviors and belief systems, if things feel out of alignment in your life.

Breathe
Devote a few minutes of your day to breathing and relaxing

Journaling
Stay connected with your thoughts and emotions by writing them

Gratitude
Practicing gratitude helps in grounding you and your emotion

Movement
Get your body to move throughout the day and rejuvenate

Don't you know that you yourselves are God's temple and that God's Spirit dwells in your midst?

~ 1 Corinthians 3:16(NIV)

Self-Care

Week One
Mental Health
Start your journey into wellness by working on your mind!
☐

Week Two
Adulting
It's time to take control of your schedule and get stuff done!
☐

Week Three
Relationships
This week, foster relationships that bring you joy and happiness
☐

Week Four
Nutrition
Focus on eating intuitively and getting rid of guilt related to food
☐

Week Five
Fitness
Get your body moving and endorphins rushing this week!
☐

Week Six
Skin+Haircare
It's time to slap on your favorite face and hair mask! Pamper yourself!
☐

Do you not know that your bodies are temple of the Holy Spirit, who is in you, whom you have received from God? You are not your own; you were bought at price. Therefore, honor God with your bodies.

~1 Corinthians 6:19-20 (NIV)

Self Care

Stretch all your muscles	Drink 8 glasses of water	Spend time with nature	Eat your favorite treat	Go to bed early
Listen to your favorite playlist	Take a relaxing bath	Cry it out	Eat your favorite meal	Go to bed on time
Take yourself on a date	Journaling	Pamper yourself	Practice gratitude	Try something new
Explore a new cafe	Plan a day out with your loved ones	Meditate for 15 minutes	Digital Detox	Read your favorite book
Be kind to a stranger	Make time to exercise	Cook a healthy meal	Make a moodboard	Watch the sunset
Do nothing today	Re-watch your favorite movie	Create a vision board	Practice Self-Compassion	Try to think and talk poitively

Six days you shall labor, but on the seventh day you shall rest; even during the plowing season and harvest you must rest. ~Exodus 34:21 (NIV)

Self-Care Challenge

For each day this month, spend 20 minutes completing a daily self-care related task. Once you've completed the task, check the relevant day's checkbox.

Day 1 ☐	Day 11 ☐	Day 21 ☐
Day 2 ☐	Day 12 ☐	Day 22 ☐
Day 3 ☐	Day 13 ☐	Day 23 ☐
Day 4 ☐	Day 14 ☐	Day 24 ☐
Day 5 ☐	Day 15 ☐	Day 25 ☐
Day 6 ☐	Day 16 ☐	Day 26 ☐
Day 7 ☐	Day 17 ☐	Day 27 ☐
Day 8 ☐	Day 18 ☐	Day 28 ☐
Day 9 ☐	Day 19 ☐	Day 29 ☐
Day 10 ☐	Day 20 ☐	Day 30 ☐

Very early in the morning, while it was still dark, Jesus got up, left the house and went off to a solitary place, where he prayed.

~Mark 1:35 (NIV)

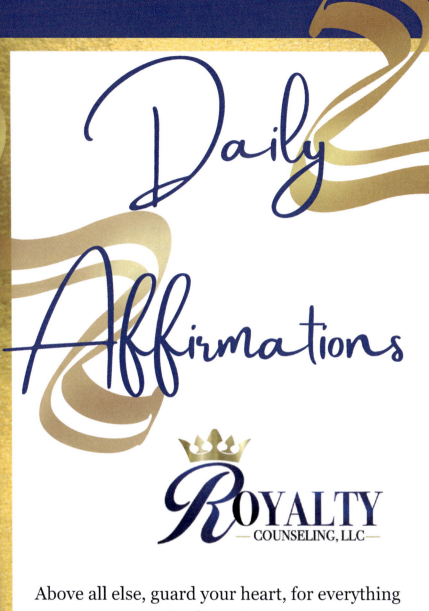

Word: STRENGTH

Scripture: GOD IS OUR REFUGE & STRENGTH, AND PRESENT HELP IN TROUBLE.

Affirmation: I AM STRONG

Word: COURAGE

Scripture: BE STRONG AND COURAGEOUS. DO NOT BE TERRIFIED; DO NOT BE DISCOURAGED, FOR THE LORD YOU GOD IS WITH YOUR WHEREVER YOU GO.

Affirmation: I AM COURAGOUS

Word: REST

Scripture: COME TO ME, ALL YOU WHO ARE WEARY & BURDENED, AND I WILL GIVE YOU REST.

Affirmation: I AM WELL RESTED

Word: WORRY FREE

Scripture: GIVE ALL YOUR WORRIES AND CARES TO GOD FOR HE CARES ABOUT YOU.

Affirmation: I AM WORRY FREE

Word: WINNER

Scripture: I CAN DO ALL THINGS THROUGH CHRIST WHO STRENGTHENS ME.

Affirmation: I AM WINNER

Word: HUMBLE

Scripture: HUMBLE YOURSELF BEFORE THE LORD AND HE WILL LIFT YOU UP.

Affirmation: I AM HUMBLE

Word: FAITH

Scripture: NOW FAITH IS THE SUBSTANCE OF THINGS HOPED FOR, AND THE EVIDENCE OF THINGS NOT SEEN.

Affirmation: I AM A PERSON OF GREAT FAITH

Word: FAITH WALK

Scripture: WE WALK BY FAITH AND NOT BY SIGHT.

Affirmation: I AM A FAITH WALKER

Word: JOYFUL

Scripture: ALWAYS BE JOYFUL, PRAY CONTINUALLY, AND GIVE THANKS IN ALL CIRCUMSTANCES.

Affirmation: I AM JOYFUL

Word: PRAY

Scripture: PRAY MORE. WORRY LESS

Affirmation: I AM PRAYERFUL

Word: CHILD/CHILDREN

Scripture: CHILDREN ARE A GIFT FROM THE LORD. THEY ARE A REWARD FROM HIM.

Affirmation: I LOVE MY CHILDREN. THEY ARE THE PERFECT GIFT FROM GOD

Word: LOVED

Scripture: LOVE NEVER FAILS

Affirmation: I AM LOVED

Card 1

Word: LOVE

Scripture: LOVE DOES NOT KEEP A RECORD OF WRONGS. IT DOES NOT DELIGHT IN EVIL. IT REJOICES IN THE TRUTH. LOVE PROTECTS, TRUSTS, AND PRESERVES.

Affirmation: I AM LOVED & I SHOW LOVE

Card 2

Words: LOVE & KINDNESS

Scripture: LOVE IS PATIENT; LOVE IS KIND. IT DOES NOT ENVY OR BOAST. IT'S NOT PROUD, RUDE, SELF-SEEKING AND IT DOE'S NOT EASILY ANGER.

Affirmation: I AM A LOVING & KIND

Card 3

Word: PROSPEROUS

Scripture: FOR I KNOW THE PLANS I HAVE FOR YOU. PLANS TO PROSPER YOU AND NOT HARM YOU, PLANS TO GIVE YOU HOPE AND A FUTURE.

Affirmation: I AM PROSPEROUS

Card 4

Word: LONG SUFFERING

Scripture: WE REJOICE IN OUR SUFFERINGS BECAUSE WE KNOW SUFFERING PRODUCES PERSEVERANCE, CHARACTER, AND HOPE.

Affirmation: I AM ABLE TO HANDLE STRESS WELL I AM STRESS-FREE

Card 5

Word: PEOPLE BUILDER

Scripture: ENCOURAGE ONE ANOTHER AND BUILD EACH OTHER UP.

Affirmation: I AM A PEOPLE BUILDER

Card 6

Word: ANGER FREE

Scripture: BE QUICK TO LISTEN, SLOW TO SPEAK, AND SLOW TO BECOME ANGRY.

Affirmation: I AM FREE FROM ANGER

Word: MARRIAGE
Scripture: THEREFORE WHAT GOD HAS JOINED TOGETHER, LET NO ONE SEPARATE.
Affirmation: I AM HAPPILY MARRIED

Word: HOPE
Scripture: AND NOW, THESE THREE REMAIN: FAITH, HOPE, AND LOVE. BUT THE GREATEST OF THESE IS LOVE.
Affirmation: I AM FULL OF HOPE

Word: PURPOSE
Scripture: PERHAPS YOU WERE BORN FOR SUCH A TIME AS THIS.
Affirmation: I LIVE IN MY PURPOSE

Word: THANKFUL
Scripture: GIVE THANKS IN ALL CIRCUMSTANCES, FOR THIS IS GOD'S WILL FOR YOU IN CHRIST JESUS.
Affirmation: I AM THANKFUL

Word: RIGHTEOUS
Scripture: THE RIGHTEOUS WILL SHINE LIKE THE SUN IN THE KINGDOM OF THEIR FATHER.
Affirmation: I AM RIGHTEOUS

Word: ALWAYS SAFE
Scripture: FOR THE LORD GIVES HIS ANGELS CHARGE OVER THEE, TO KEEP THEE IN ALL THY WAYS.
Affirmation: I AM ALWAYS SAFE

Word: HEALING

Scripture: YOUR LIGHT WILL BREAK FORTH LIKE THE DAWN, AND YOUR HEALING WILL QUICKLY APPEAR.

Affirmation: I HAVE GODS HEALING POWER

Word: HEALED

Scripture: I HAVE HEARD YOUR PRAYER AND SEEN YOUR TEARS. I WILL HEAL YOU.

Affirmation: I AM HEALED

Word: CARE FREE

Scripture: CAST YOUR CARES ON THE LORD, AND HE WILL SUSTAIN YOU; HE WILL NEVER LET THE RIGHTEOUS BE SHAKEN.

Affirmation: I AM CARE FREE

Word: HEALED HEART

Scripture: HE HEALS THE BROKENHEARTED AND BINDS UP THEIR WOUNDS.

Affirmation: MY HEART IS HEALED

Words: HEALED AND WHOLE

Scripture: BY HIS STRIPES I AM HEALED.

Affirmation: I AM HEALED & WHOLE

Word: SOUND MIND

Scripture: FOR GOD HAS NOT GIVEN US A SPIRIT OF FEAR BUT OF POWER AND OF LOVE AND OF A SOUND MIND.

Affirmation: I HAVE A SOUND MIND

Word: WISDOM AND KNOWLEDGE

Scripture: WISDOM AND KNOWLEDGE HAVE BEEN GRANTED TO YOU. I WILL GIVE YOU RICHES, WEALTH AND HONOR, SUCH AS NONE OF THE KINGS WHO WERE BEFORE YOU HAS PROSPERED NOR THOSE WHO WILL COME AFTER YOU.

Affirmation: I AM WISE AND KNOWLEDGABLE

Word: WEALTH

Scripture: BUT YOU SHALL REMEMBER THE LORD YOUR GOD, FOR IT IS HE WHO GIVES YOU THE POWER TO MAKE WEALTH, THAT HE MAY CONFIRM HIS COVENANT WHICH HE SWORE TO YOUR FATHER, AS IT IS THIS DAY.

Affirmation: I AM WEALTHY

Word: BLESSED

Scripture: THE BLESSING OF THE LORD BRINGS WEALTH, WITHOUT PAINFUL TOIL FOR IT.

Affirmation: I AM BLESSED

Word: PROTECTION

Scripture: GOD IS OUR REFUGE AND STRENGTH AND HELP IN TROUBLE; THEREFORE, WE WILL NOT FEAR.

Affirmation: I AM PROTECTED BY GOD

Word: HELP

Scripture: THE LORD IS GOOD, A STRONGHOLD: AND HE KNOWS THOSE WHO TRUST IN HIM.

Affirmation: I HAVE A GREAT HELPER

Word: SAFETY

Scripture: NO DISASTER CAN OVERTAKE YOU OR PLAGUE COME NEAR YOUR TENT. HE HAS GIVEN HIS ANGELS ORDERS ABOUT YOU TO GUARD YOU WHEREVER YOU GO.

Affirmation: I HAVE A SAFE PLACE

Word: PEACE

Scripture: IN PEACE, I WILL LIE DOWN AND FALL ASLEEP, FOR YOU ALONE LORD MAKE ME SECURE.

Affirmation: I LIVE A LIFE FULL OF PEACE

Word: STILL

Scripture: BE STILL AND KNOW THAT I AM GOD.

Affirmation: I AM STILL, QUIET, AND IN PERFECT PEACE

Word: TRUST

Scripture: TRUST IN THE LORD GOD WITH ALL YOUR HEART AND LEAN NOT ON YOUR OWN UNDERSTANDING: IN ALL YOUR WAYS SUBMIT TO HIM, AND HE WILL MAKE YOUR PATHS STRAIGHT.

Affirmation: I TRUST GOD

Words: FAMILY FAVOR

Scripture: HER CHILDREN ARISE AND CALL HER BLESSED; HER HUSBAND ALSO, AND HE PRAISES HER.

Affirmation: MY KIDS & HUSBAND LOVE ME

Word: RIGHTEOUS

Scripture: I'VE NEVER SEEN THE RIGHTEOUS FORSAKEN, NOR HIS SEED BEGGING FOR BREAD.

Affirmation: I AM THE RIGHTEOUSNESS OF GOD

Words: ALWAYS SAFE

Scripture: FOR THE LORD GIVES HIS ANGELS CHARGE OVER THEE, TO KEEP THEE IN ALL THY WAYS.

Affirmation: I AM ALWAYS SAFE

HOW TO BE
Kind to Yourself

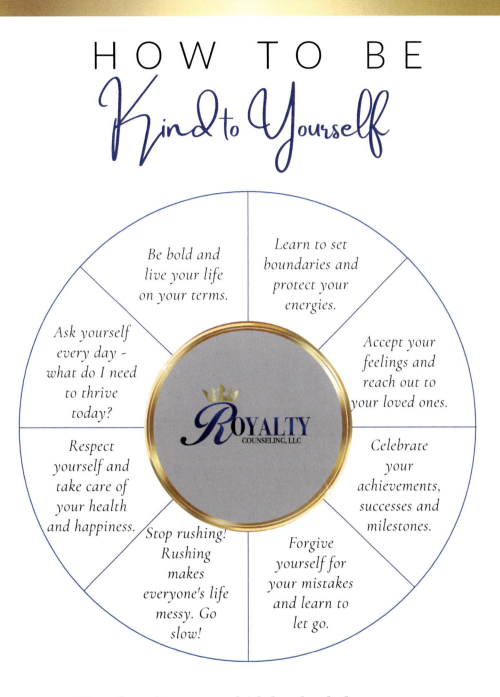

- Be bold and live your life on your terms.
- Learn to set boundaries and protect your energies.
- Ask yourself every day - what do I need to thrive today?
- Accept your feelings and reach out to your loved ones.
- Respect yourself and take care of your health and happiness.
- Celebrate your achievements, successes and milestones.
- Stop rushing! Rushing makes everyone's life messy. Go slow!
- Forgive yourself for your mistakes and learn to let go.

Daughter/Son, your faith has healed you.
Go in peace and be freed from your suffering.

~Mark 5:34 (NIV)

JOURNAL HOW TO BE *Kind to Yourself*

My grace is sufficient for you, for my power is made perfect in weakness.
~ 2 Corinthians 12:9 (NIV)

I would love to collaborate. Share pictures of you using your journal/workbook and success stories about your career or your business.

Inbox, e-mail, or DM us a selfie, picture, or video of you with your new journal. Let us know how you love it and how you use it.
We love testimonials'.

Heyyy Family, Let's Write Your Future, Set Goals, Plan and Let's Refresh and be Trauma Free. Write your Dreams, See God's Success Manifest in Your Life, Career, and Business.

STAY CONNECTED TO LAKEISHA POPE
MENTAL HEALTH THERAPIST & COACH

- ✉ Keisha@royaltycounselingllc.com
- 🌐 www.royaltycounselingllc.com
- 📷 rcounselingllc
- ⓕ LaKeisha Pope-Royalty Counseling

Made in the USA
Middletown, DE
27 June 2024

56413708R00027